VOICES IN MY HEAD, GOD IN MY HEART

A Journey of Identify, Faith and Freedom the A.U.N.T.I.E.™ Way

SHERIE RANDOLPH-DUNHAM

(Auntie Ree)

Table of Contents

DEDICATION

To **my husband**, Shawn Dunham

This year, 2025 is extra special because it marks 40 years when we first met that first hot summer in 1985. You have consistently given me the encouragement to find my voice and the courage to speak it. Through every season — the brokenness, the beauty, the growth — you've been there.

Thank you for loving me through my becoming and reminding me that I married my best friend.

With all my love, Ree to With all My Luv, Ree

To **you**, the reader —

May these pages be a mirror, a guide, and a gentle push toward your own healing, freedom, and faith. If you have ever felt unseen, unloved, or unheard this is for you. You are not forgotten. You are not broken. You are becoming.

This is more than a book – It's a breakthrough and welcome to the T.E.A.M. Luv movement and journey.

Auntie Ree

Preface

This book is more than pages and paragraphs — it's a piece of my soul, wrapped in truth, healing, and purpose. I didn't write this for fame or followers. I wrote it for *you*. For the young woman carrying silent shame. For the young man struggling to find identity. For every person who's ever felt like the black sheep — unseen, unheard, unloved, and misunderstood.

There was a time when I didn't think I'd survive my story. Trauma, addiction, rejection, identity confusion, and deep wounds from those who were supposed to love me — I carried it all. And yet, by God's grace, I'm still standing. Not because I had it all together, but because I finally chose to tell the truth, trust the process, and let God transform my pain into purpose.

Through my A.U.N.T.I.E.™ framework — **Acknowledge your pain, Uncover truth, Nurture your spirit, Trust the process, Inspire, and Empower** — I discovered the path to wholeness. This is the same path I now walk boldly as Auntie Ree, and the same path I pray will guide you to your own breakthrough. These steps helped me silence shame, stand in my truth, and walk boldly in purpose.

I wrote *Voices in My Head, God in My Heart*: A Journey of Identity, Faith and Freedom for every person who's ever struggled with identity, faith, and the fear of not being enough.

If you're reading this, know that it's not by accident. God has a plan for your life. And whether you're in the middle of the mess or on the edge of your miracle, I want you to lean in. Let these words remind you that you matter, you are loved, and you are not alone.

My prayer is that as you read, you'll hear God's voice louder than your doubts — and begin your own journey of healing, identity, faith, and freedom.

With love & truth,

Sherie Randolph-Dunham (Auntie Ree)

INTRODUCTION:

The Real Power of an AUNTIE

There's something sacred about the presence of an AUNTIE.

Not just the woman who shows up at the cookout with the loudest laugh and the warmest hugs—but the real AUNTIE. The kind who carries stories in her scars. The kind who's walked through fire, but came out with a word, not just for herself, but for the next generation. AUNTIES like that don't just speak—they pour.

They don't just correct—they cover. They don't just advise—they advance you.

I am that AUNTIE.

I am AUNTIE Ree.

This book ain't about perfection—it's about perspective. The kind of perspective you only gain when you've been through some thangs. I've battled identity confusion, drug addiction, attempted suicide, sexual abuse, divorce, and so many other things that tried to silence me. I've stood in mirrors I didn't recognize, lived in relationships that numbed me, and cried out to a God I wasn't even sure heard me.

But He did. And I made it. Not just through—but transformed.

And now? I'm here to give it back. To pass the baton with truth, transparency, and Luv. This book is my offering to you—my younger sisters and brothers trying to find yourselves in a world that keeps trying to define you before you ever get to discover who you really are.

This is for every young soul trying to understand their identity—emotionally, sexually, spiritually.

For every teen who's ever felt torn between who they are, who they think they should be, and who the world expects them to become. For every college student secretly suffering in silence while smiling on the surface.

This book is for you.

The A.U.N.T.I.E.™ Method—Acknowledge your feelings. Uncover your truth. Nurture your spirit. Trust the process. Inspire. Empower. — This isn't just a trademark or a title. It's my testimony. It's the steps I took when the mask had to come off and the healing had to begin.

I didn't write this to go viral. I wrote this to go vital—to speak life to the lost, strength to the scared, and vision to the ones who've forgotten how to dream. If my journey can help you avoid a pitfall, embrace your truth earlier, or walk with your head a little higher—then every chapter is worth it.

We're in this together, Baby. This is the AUNTIE way.

Real. Raw. Redeemed.

Let's walk it out—chapter by chapter.

From pain to purpose.

From questions to clarity.

From surviving to becoming the YOU, you were always meant to be.

With deep Luv and Truth,

AUNTIE Ree

Founder of the A.U.N.T.I.E.™ Methodology

CHAPTER 1:

Acknowledge Your Feelings

"Before you figure out who you are, you've got to be honest about what hurt you."

Let's start with the truth:

Most of us didn't choose to be confused. We were conditioned to be. We don't always intentionally suppress our childhood traumas. It's not like we sat down one day and said, "I'm going to pretend none of this happened." No, it happens in pieces—quietly, slowly, like dust settling over memories too painful to face. One little lie at a time. One fake smile at a time. One "I'm good" when we're really not.

But here's the thing about suppressed pain—it doesn't stay hidden. It leaks. It shows up in how we act, how we love, how we treat ourselves. That's why by the time you hit your teenage years or early adulthood; you're sitting there trying to figure out why you feel off all the time. Why do you show up for everybody, but still feel invisible? Why you're always asking, "Why am I like this?" and can't quite connect the dots.

The Quiet Crisis

You might feel comfortable being the loud, goofy one around your friends or the one who gives good advice. Or the one who always makes sure everybody else is straight. But it's in the quiet moments—when you lay your head on the pillow and the room is dark—that it hits you:

"I know there's more to me than this."

"This can't be who God intended me to be."

And that right there... that whisper in the dark... is the beginning of your real identity trying to break through.

Disconnection Feels Like Identity Loss

You start feeling disconnected from yourself. You're not sure if the version of you that people luv is the real you—or just the version you created so people wouldn't leave and if you're naturally introverted like I was, you go even deeper into isolation. You start shrinking. You stop sharing. You tell yourself nobody would understand anyway, so what's the point? Here's what I need you to know: what you're feeling is real. And it matters.

You are not overreacting.

You are not being dramatic.

You are hurting.

You are questioning.

You are searching for the real you under everything life forced you to become.

Why Do I Luv So Hard?

There's another layer to the confusion that hits young people with big hearts.

You ask yourself:

"Why do I give the shirt off my back to people who wouldn't do the same for me?"

"Why am I always the one checking in on others, but nobody checks on me?"

"Why does it seem like the better I do, the more I get hated?"

And then comes the identity conflict—you start wondering if something is wrong with you.

You try to adjust. You try to be tougher. You try to care less.

But that isn't you. That's your trauma trying to protect you from the same kind of pain you never deserved in the first place.

Family Was My First Hurt

Let me be transparent. The majority of my first wounds came from family. I was taught that "blood is thicker than water," so I tried to believe that. I tried to believe that loyalty to your family meant you had to stay silent when they hurt you, but let me tell you something: family doesn't get a free pass to break you.

I was told that "family can do things to you because things were done to them." For a while, I accepted that. Until I realized that the same pain that shaped them was now shaping me—and I had to make a choice.

Do I keep the cycle going or do I break it? The silence doesn't heal. It hides and I was tired of hiding.

At a very early age, I dealt with colorism, sexual abuse, jealousy—all from the hands of people who were supposed to protect me. They shattered

13

me. It left me walking around in a fog, trying to figure out who I was—without realizing that my identity had been bruised before I even had a chance to form one.

Acknowledge It, Don't Escape It

See, here's what nobody tells you:

You can't heal what you don't first acknowledge.

You'll keep trying to build an identity around your pain instead of around your truth.

You'll keep switching friend groups, clothes, genders, pronouns, dreams, and beliefs, hoping that one day it finally feels right—but it won't if it's just a mask covering a wound you never gave permission to breathe.

So, this chapter is the first step in the A.U.N.T.I.E.™ Method:

Acknowledge Your Feelings.

Feel it.

Don't fix it yet.

Don't explain it away.

Just name it.

Say:

"I feel abandoned."

"I feel confused."

"I feel invisible."

14

"I feel angry."

"I feel scared of who I'm becoming."

That's where it starts.

It's Not Too Late to Come Back to You

You are not too far gone.

You are not too broken.

You are not too weird, too different, too anything.

You are just hurt. And that's okay.

What you cannot do—what I refuse to let you do—is stay in that place and call it your identity.

You don't have to keep carrying pain that doesn't belong to you.

You don't have to keep being who they told you to be.

You don't have to make yourself small just so other people feel big.

It's time to come back to you.

Your Turn: Starts Here

Here's your first assignment, Baby:

1. Sit with your feelings. Don't scroll past them.

   Ask yourself: What have I been feeling that I've been scared to say out loud?

2. Write a letter to the younger you.

Let them know you see their pain. Let them know they didn't deserve it. Let them know it's okay to cry.

3. Say this out loud, even if you don't believe it yet:

    "My feelings matter. My pain is real. But it doesn't define who I am."

This is your first step toward healing your identity.

Not by changing who you are, but by finally facing what hurt you.

You're not alone.

You're not weak.

You're becoming.

CHAPTER 2:

Uncover Your Truth – When Labels Lie

You'll never find yourself in a label that was meant to limit you.

L et's get something straight to the jump, identity isn't a costume. It isn't something you throw on 'cause its trending. It definitely isn't a label that someone else stuck on you when you were too broken or confused to say otherwise, but that's what happens, right?

You go through something...

You carry pain that nobody sees...

You learn to survive instead of live...

Before you even get a chance to discover who you really are — The world hands you a label and tells you to wear it like it fits.

Urban Identity Crisis is Real

Let's talk about it. You grew up in the world

Where **"LIKES"** validate your worth.

Where sexuality is fluid, but emotions are suffocating.

Where everybody wants to be seen, but nobody feels understood.

Where gender, image, style, and status are up for grabs—but your soul? That stays hidden.

Today's youth are battling more identity confusion than ever before:

- **Sexual identity crisis:** "Am I this way, or did trauma shape me into this?"

- **Spiritual identity crisis:** "Is there really a God? And if so, does He even see me?"

- **Cultural identity crisis:** "Am I acting white if I speak proper? Am I Black enough if I don't fit the stereotype?"

- **Emotional identity crisis:** "Why do I always feel numb? Am I depressed or just surviving?"

- **Relational identity crisis:** "If my own family didn't luv me right, how do I even know what luv looks like?"

It's hard to figure out who you are when you've been taught to become what makes everyone else comfortable.

Baby, the moment you start lying to yourself is the moment you start dying a slow death inside and I don't want that for you.

The Truth Behind My Desire

Let me tell you something personal. I didn't always have a close, personal relationship with God. I knew about God; I believed in Him... but I didn't walk with Him.

Still, I'd hear people say, "Something told me..."

Nah, that something? That was God.

That whisper, that feeling, that gut check—it was Him trying to get my attention, but when you've been through the kind of trauma I endured, it gets hard to hear anything over the pain.

Between the ages of 5 and 7, I was sexually abused. When I was 16 my mother was involved with an older man who also tried to touch me in inappropriate ways. No child should have to go through that, but I did. That trauma planted a seed in me — a deep confusion about my body, my worth, and my desire.

I had family members and friends in same-sex relationships that I never judged because that wasn't my spirit. But me? I kept my thoughts in the dark, wrapped in shame, because I didn't understand them. I didn't understand me.

The Breaking Point

I didn't act on those desires until I was 30 years old. Up until then, I had been in a 13-year relationship with my best friend. The father of my 9-year-old daughter. It was always just us three. That was my world.

But the struggle?

The struggle was real.

We went through everything—bankruptcy, homelessness, heartbreak.

Not because of cheating or abuse, but because life just wore us out.

The dream got too heavy.

The money dried up.

The pressure cracked what luv tried to hold together.

So, when that relationship ended, I was tired. Tired of fighting. Tired of trying. So, in my tiredness, I told myself: "I can do bad all by myself."

Even though the weight of financial stress was heavy, it was the years of unspoken mental and emotional abuse that finally cracked the foundation of my marriage. Thirteen years with my childhood sweetheart... and it all came crashing down. That divorce wasn't just a legal ending—it was the moment when the seeds of unresolved trauma, long buried, began to claw their way to the surface.

In the quiet aftermath, I sat with my pain, trying to make sense of it all. But here's the truth most people won't tell you: when your mind has been warped by emotional warfare, you don't see life clearly. You don't process luv clearly. Trauma distorts your lens. You start questioning everything—your worth, your identity, your desires. I started believing the lie that maybe I was meant to be with a woman. This wasn't because I had clarity—but because I was drowning in confusion. That's how deep the manipulation and internal damage had gone. So, I entered a same-sex relationship, searching for healing in a place that only gave me more of the same—more dysfunction, more toxicity, more abuse. It wasn't luv or liberation. It was trauma trying to relive itself in a different costume. When your emotional compass is broken, even pain starts to feel like comfort.

So, I acted on what I had been hiding. Not because I was chasing truth— but because I was chasing relief. And I thought maybe... just maybe... this would give me what I had been missing.

Here's what I learned the hard way:

Relief is not the same as peace. Escaping pain is not the same as embracing purpose. What I uncovered during that season was this:

Those same-sex desires?

They didn't come from freedom. They came from my wounds and Baby, no identity built on pain can ever bring you peace. The truth I uncovered wasn't just about my sexuality. It was about my spiritual identity. I didn't need another person to validate me. I didn't need another relationship to prove something. I needed GOD and not just religion or just a church or not even just a scripture. I needed the truth that could finally silence all the lies I'd been living.

And that truth was this:

I was not what happened to me.

I was not who I slept with.

I was not the version of myself I created to cope.

I was God's daughter.

Confused, yes.

Wounded, yes.

But chosen.

And the moment I started walking in truth instead of labels... I started coming back to life.

Your Truth May Hurt—But It Will Heal You

So let me ask you:

What's your truth?

Not the one you show on social media.

Not the one you created to survive your home life, your trauma, your heartbreak.

I mean the real, raw truth that you whisper to yourself in the dark.

You'll never find peace wearing a lie, but when you uncover your truth—no matter how messy it feels—you open the door to freedom. Don't be afraid of what you find because God can handle it. He already knows. He just wants you to know it, too—so you can stop living in the shadows of labels that were never yours to begin with.

Reflection: Time to Uncover

1. What label have you accepted that doesn't fully represent who you are?

2. Where do you think your identity struggles really began? Childhood? Peer pressure? Trauma?

3. What would your life look like if you started telling yourself the truth—even if it scared you?

You don't have to have all the answers today, but you do have to stop lying to yourself. Your freedom doesn't come from faking it. It comes from facing it.

With bold Luv and grace,

– AUNTIE Ree

CHAPTER 3:

Nurture Your Spirit – The Soul Behind the Selfie

"If you don't know your soul, the world will sell you an identity and convince you it's who you are."

Let's be real...

You can have the best drip, the cleanest IG grid, and followers all over the place—and still feel empty when the lights go off.

It's not that you're lost. It's that your soul is starving.

We live in a generation that's always scrolling, always comparing, always performing... and almost never pausing to check in with our spirit. We know how to filter our faces, but not our feelings. We chase vibes but can't identify what's really vibrating inside of us.

And that, Baby, is where the identity crisis starts.

Disconnected in a Connected World

You might not say it out loud, but you feel it.

You feel a little hollow, even when you're surrounded by people.

You smile on Snap but feel sad in silence.

You're motivated by aesthetics but secretly struggling with anxiety.

And the worst part?

Nobody teaches us how to fix it.

Not the schools.

Not social media.

Sometimes not even our families.

We're taught how to look the part, not how to live with peace. Let me tell you something that nobody told me when I was your age. If you don't nurture your spirit, your identity will be shaped by everything BUT your truth.

My Early Spiritual Journey (or Lack of One)

I wasn't born and raised in the church and if you're from the Northeast or anywhere outside the Bible Belt like I was, you probably weren't either. Back in the '70s, '80s, and early '90s, a lot of us didn't grow up in church families. Church wasn't the center of our world—it was something you saw on TV or visited when someone died.

I remember those white church buses that would roll through the hood and scoop up the neighborhood kids. I'd go by myself without parents or grandparents.

Even though I was young—7 or 8 years old—I felt something in those moments. I didn't understand it fully, but I knew it was warm. It was safe. It was different and I never forgot that feeling. Life has a way of distracting you from the one thing that could actually help you heal.

Church Trauma is Real Too

I tried to go back when I was 20, pregnant, and scared out of my mind. I was wrestling with the thought of abortion, and I didn't know what to do. I was lost and searching, but just when I thought I found peace in a church community, the Pastor—the same one I was looking up to—got caught cheating on his wife with young girls. That broke me and I didn't realize I had been worshipping the Pastor, not God. So, I left. Not just the church—but my hope and I stayed gone for seven years. Every time I tried to reconnect, it felt forced. I didn't last long. A few months, maybe. My spirit wanted God, but my heart was scared to trust people again.

Spiritual Rock Bottom

Then came the storm...

My 13-year marriage had failed.

I had tried a same-sex relationship hoping maybe that was what I'd been missing. But that too was filled with toxicity—emotional abuse, mental abuse, and eventually physical abuse. I was back at rock bottom, holding onto a version of myself that no longer made sense. My daughter was 12 and I looked at her, then at myself, and I said, "Something has to change."

I remember it clearly — New Year's Eve, 2002.

I hadn't stepped inside a church in five years.

But that whole day, I kept hearing:

Go to church. It wasn't a voice from the sky. It was that same warm feeling I had as a little girl sitting on that church bus. That whisper. That pull. That push.

That was God.

I flushed an entire bag of cocaine down the toilet, packed up my daughter and we went to church! Yes, just like that.

And Baby... I never looked back.

Rebuilding from the Inside Out

That night, I didn't just attend a service. I surrendered.

I rededicated my life to God—the same God I accepted at 9 and got baptized for at 20. But this time was different. This time I wasn't coming to Him because I was scared. I was coming to Him because I was empty—and I finally understood that nothing else could fill me but Him.

And guess what?

My daughter accepted Christ, got baptized and we started rebuilding our lives — not from Instagram posts or TikTok trends... but from the inside out.

That was 23 years ago.

And I've never lapsed in my walk since.

This Ain't Religion—It's Restoration

Let me say this to you:

This chapter ain't about religion or rules. It's not about being perfect or performing for some church people who judge you while hiding their own mess. This chapter is about restoration.

It's about you taking a moment to ask:

"What does my spirit need?"

Not what your friends think.

Not what your IG feed promotes.

Not what the culture glamorizes, but what your soul needs. If your spirit is starving, nothing you do on the outside will ever satisfy you.

Nurturing Your Spirit Today

Here's how you can start:

1. Unplug to connect.

    •   Take a few minutes every day with no phone.

    •   Just sit. Breathe. Ask your soul how it's really doing.

2. Talk to God in your own voice.

    •   You don't need fancy words.

    •   Just be real. Say, "God, I don't know what I'm doing. But I want to get closer to You."

3. Feed your spirit, not just your scroll.

    •   Read something that uplifts you.

    •   Listen to music that makes you feel whole, not hollow.

4. Stop chasing peace from people.

- They can't give you what they didn't create.

- Peace comes from within. It comes from a connection with the Creator.

Final Word from Your AUNTIE

You won't find your identity in a selfie.

You won't discover your purpose in a post.

You won't build real joy from fake followers.

The soul behind the selfie matters and when you nurture your spirit, you begin to hear your own voice above the noise. You begin to feel God again and Baby, when God starts speaking to your spirit, the world can't silence your worth.

With soul-deep Luv,

– AUNTIE Ree

CHAPTER 4:

Trust the Process – Becoming Through the Breaking

"Sometimes your identity isn't found in what you do—it's revealed in what you survive."

I want to start this chapter by saying something you might not hear often enough:

You're not crazy. You're not broken. You're not weak. You're in process.

And trust me, that sh*t is messy.

Let me tell you something that isn't easy to say out loud, but it's true:

Most of the pain I've endured in life wasn't punishment, it was preparation.

And it took me a long time to trust that. See, identity isn't built when everything is going right. It's built when life falls apart and you gotta figure out who you are without the titles, the followers, or the filters.

Let's talk about the breaking point.

I've faced so many moments in life where I honestly didn't think I was gonna make it:

- Laying on the abortion table—twice—and walking away both times with tears in my eyes and a baby in my belly.

- Being so lost in postpartum depression that I tried to end my life with pills when my daughter was just two months old.

- Falling asleep at the wheel with my baby in the backseat—waking up just before crashing, flipping the car three times and walking away without a scratch.

- Selling cocaine to make ends meet.

- Filing bankruptcy—twice.

- Homeless—eight times.

- Facing five years in prison for assaulting a police officer.

- Doing jail time for reckless driving and D.U.I.

- Drug use and almost overdosing.

- Living with high blood pressure since 19, battling migraines for 40 years, and surviving carbon monoxide poisoning.

- Being fired the same day I injured my knee at work—and fighting tooth and nail just to get the surgery I needed.

- Going through perimenopause for 7 years and dealing with depression so deep I didn't care if I lived or died.

But guess what?

God didn't let it kill me. He used every single breakdown to build something in me.

And if you're still breathing? That means He isn't done with you either.

The Lie That Felt Like Home

For years, I called a lie home because it was the only place I ever felt safe. Let me say that again. I found comfort in confusion because comfort was the only thing I craved.

After years of chaos.

After the abuse.

After the drugs.

After trying to die by suicide.

After watching my father kill my grandfather.

After never feeling enough for the world or myself.

I just wanted to feel something that didn't hurt. So, when I fell into a relationship with a woman, I felt seen. I felt held. I felt like somebody finally "got me." Even in those moments of closeness, there was still a silent scream inside of me — a whisper from my soul saying:

"This still ain't it."

I ignored it. Why? Because the pain of staying seemed less scary than the pain of changing.

The Process is Where the Real You is Born

You don't grow in the spotlight—you grow in the shadows.

It's in the quiet breakdowns, the sleepless nights, the silent tears... that's where your true self starts to emerge, but trusting the process doesn't mean you won't hurt. It means you'll keep moving even when you do.

So, if you're going through it right now, and it feels like your life is on fire—don't run.

Let it burn what wasn't meant to stay.

Your identity is being revealed in the rubble. You're becoming.

Reflection Points:

1. What have you survived that you never gave yourself credit for?

   Don't minimize your story—what you walked through shaped something strong in you.

2. Have you ever felt like giving up on yourself? What made you keep going?

   Dig into those moments. There's power in the fact that you're still here.

3. What part of your life right now feels like it's falling apart?

   Could it be that something new is trying to be born through the breaking?

Final Word from Your AUNTIE:

Baby, trust me—your breakdowns are not the end of you. They're the opening. They're the cracks where the light sneaks in. I know pain intimately, but I also know what it feels like to rise from it with power.

Don't rush the process. Don't run from the pressure. Diamonds are formed there.

Trust that God is using everything—yes, even that—to bring the real you forward.

With enduring Luv,

– AUNTIE Ree

CHAPTER 5:

Inspire – Turning Your Story Into Someone Else's Survival Guide

"You didn't go through all that just to keep quiet about it."

Young people—listen to me.

What you've survived can save somebody else, but only if you're willing to share it. I used to hide my scars.

Ashamed of the jail time.

Ashamed of the drug use.

Ashamed of the same-sex relationship.

Ashamed that I'd been divorced... that I'd been suicidal... that I'd failed over and over again.

But now?

I speak with boldness because somebody, somewhere is going through the same hell I went through—and they need to know it's possible to come out.

Your Truth Can Light Up Someone's Darkness

We're in a generation that's starving for real.

Not another influencer.

Not another "perfect" image.

But someone who's been in the dirt and came out clean—with a message that says, "You can too."

That's what your story is: a light in someone else's tunnel. Maybe your past isn't picture perfect. Neither is mine, but if God could use me—this girl who tried to take her own life, spent nights in jail, who did hard drugs, who walked through hell with high heels and a prayer—He can use you.

Don't Be Afraid to Speak

You don't need a stage to inspire.

You don't need a mic or a brand or a blue check.

All you need is your voice and your truth.

Speak it.

Write it.

Live it.

Your story is sacred, and somebody's survival depends on your honesty. There's something deeply broken in this generation when it comes to how we influence each other. Instead of uplifting one another, we pressure each other into silence, self-destruction, and settling for less than we're worth. What if the same energy used to dare your friend to skip class, pop a pill, or fight for clout… was used to dare them to dream bigger, heal deeper, and live with purpose?

We need to inspire each other to rise—not crash. There's already too much pain in the world, too many young lives lost before they ever knew how valuable they were. There are too many voices silenced by suicide, gun violence, drug overdoses, and depression masked behind designer clothes and fake laughs. It doesn't have to be like this.

You have the power to create a new culture. A culture where we challenge our friends to get therapy, not just turn up.

Where we encourage each other to write the book, apply for the scholarship, learn a trade, start that business, tell that truth, or break that cycle. You can be that kind of friend. That kind of light. That kind of leader.

Because truth be told? Everybody's following somebody.

So, ask yourself: What direction am I pointing people in?

Are you leading your people to pain… or purpose?

To dysfunction… or destiny?

Inspiration isn't about being perfect. It's about being real enough to show others that greatness is still possible—even after the struggle. It's about letting people see that they're not crazy for wanting more, for being different, for stepping away from what's popular to walk in what's purposeful.

This generation doesn't just need **Influencers**. It needs **Inspirers.** Be one.

Reflection Points:

1. What parts of your story have you been afraid to share? Why?

   Sometimes the thing that feels most shameful is the exact thing someone else needs to hear to survive.

2. Who is someone in your life that you could inspire just by being honest?

   Your vulnerability might be the lifeline someone is silently praying for.

3. What message do you carry that the younger version of you needed to hear?

   Speak to them. Be the voice you wish you had.

Final Word from Your AUNTIE:

You don't have to have a platform to be powerful. Your truth is enough. Your journey is enough. And your voice—especially when it's trembling—is enough. Somebody is waiting for your courage to give them permission to breathe. Don't waste your pain. Use it. Let it heal somebody else the way you're learning to heal yourself.

With deep and divine Luv,

– AUNTIE Ree

CHAPTER 6:

Empower – Taking Back Your Voice and Vision

"The world tried to name you. Now it's time for YOU to define who you are."

Let's talk about real empowerment—not the kind that's loud but shallow.

I'm talking about the kind of power that comes from healing your mind, claiming your space, and walking in your truth with your head high—even when your past tries to shame you.

Empowerment doesn't start with applause.

It doesn't come from likes, retweets, or being the most outspoken in the room.

It begins quietly—when you stop hiding from yourself.

When you decide to take ownership of your story, no matter how messy, and say, "This happened, but it doesn't define me it prepared me." See, power is born the moment you stop wishing your past was different and start working with what you've been through. Everything I survived— from being suicidal, addicted, abandoned, delivered—wasn't just for me.

It was for the people God would send my way. People like you. You empower others by showing them what healing looks like in real time. Not perfection. Not performance. Just honesty. Just showing up and saying, "If I made it, you can too."

And here's the real truth:

Your life is somebody's answered prayer. There's someone out there who is crying in the same dark place you used to live in—and your voice, your wisdom, your story might be the very light that leads them out. So, stop doubting your influence just because your journey hasn't been perfect.

The messy parts? That's where the ministry is.

The painful chapters? That's where the power lives.

When you embrace your whole self—flaws, failures, and all—you give other people permission to do the same. That's what real empowerment looks like.

And Baby, when you walk in that kind of truth, you don't just change lives—you change legacies.

I know what it feels like to be silenced, overlooked, broken and feel like everything in life has tried to strip you of your voice.

But Baby—you can get it back.

Here's How I Took Mine Back:

- I started therapy at 52. Yes, 52! And I stayed consistent from 2021–2024 until I found the right match.

- I started doing mental health check-ins every April—my birthday month—because I treat my mind like I treat my body.

- I changed my lifestyle. Got off blood pressure meds. Lost 30 pounds. Went pescatarian. Focused on sleep, movement, peace.

- I stopped performing for family who couldn't see my healing— and I let them go when they stopped speaking to me after my second book dropped.

- I leaned into my introverted nature but refused to let it stop me from walking in my purpose.

- I accepted that the anointing on my life was bigger than their approval.

And now?

I'm 56, reinventing myself, and walking in peace. I don't need to prove anything and I'm living proof that you can rise from the ashes and shine anyway.

Power Moves for Young People:

1. Start with honesty.

   - Say what you feel. Own your story. Name your pain. That's where your power begins.

2. Claim your space.

   - You belong. Even in rooms that don't look like you. Even in spaces that don't get you.

3. Build your vision.

   - Don't just let life happen—design it.

- Make goals. Speak affirmations. Write your future down like it already exists.

4. Protect your peace.

  - Not everyone deserves access.

  - Say no. Block what drains you. Prioritize rest and reflection.

5. Stay rooted in God.

  - He knows the real you. He called you. The powerful you.

  - Let Him define you—not your trauma, not your timeline, not your followers.

Reflection Points:

1. What voices in your life have tried to define your worth for you?

   It's time to rewrite that script. What do you say about yourself?

2. Where in your life do you need to reclaim your power—mentally, emotionally, and spiritually?

   Power is not control—it's clarity. Get clear on what's yours and take it back.

3. What kind of future are you dreaming of—and what small step can you take today to move toward it?

   Your vision matters. Start building it like it's already real.

Final Word from Your AUNTIE:

There's nothing more dangerous to the enemy than a young person who knows their worth. I need you to stop shrinking. Stop doubting. Stop deferring your power to people who never paid the price for it. Your life—your voice—your purpose is holy ground. Stand on it like you belong there. Because you do.

You've been through too much to stay small. You've been silent too long.

You've let the world decide your worth for far too many years.

Now it's your time.

To heal.

To rise.

To empower others just by being the most real and freed version of you.

Walk in your light, Baby.

Your story is your superpower.

With lifelong Luv and fire,

– AUNTIE Ree

CHAPTER 7:

Break the Influence – The Power to Think for Yourself

"You can't become who you were born to be while letting everyone else do the thinking for you."

Let's keep it real:

We're living in a generation that's connected to everything and everyone—except themselves.

Connected to social media, friend groups, online clout, and culture move so fast that most of us don't take time to slow down and ask one of the most important questions you'll ever ask in life:

"Is this really me?"

See, influence isn't always loud.

Sometimes it's quiet—sneaky even.

It comes in the form of a post that makes you feel like your life isn't enough.

A DM that pulls you into drama.

A group chat where everyone's doing something you know deep down isn't for you—but you go along with it anyway, because what if they stop liking you? That's the trap and it's a trap that's stealing identities every single day.

The Influence Epidemic

This generation is battling a silent identity crisis fueled by:

- **Comparison Culture:** You're constantly measuring yourself against highlight reels.

- **Peer Pressure in Disguise:** It's not just about fitting in—it's about not getting left behind.

- **Fear of Being Different:** You don't want to be the one who speaks up, steps back, or stays true—because that might cost you connection.

But Baby, let me tell you something...

There is no peace in pretending.

You weren't created to copy.

You were created to stand out—not in a flashy, "look at me" kind of way, but in a grounded, God-ordained, purpose-driven kind of way.

The Cost of Fitting In

Let's talk about what happens when you start letting other people think for you...

You start doing things you don't feel good about.

You start laughing at stuff that doesn't sit right in your spirit.

You start entertaining relationships, habits, and behaviors that slowly pull you away from your real self.

And here's the catch:

The world will always reward you for fitting in—even if it's killing your soul, but what's the point of being accepted by everyone else if you're rejecting yourself?

How to Break the Cycle

You don't need to become a rebel to break the influence.

You just need to become intentional.

Here's how:

1. Turn the phone off.

   - Not forever. But long enough to hear your own voice.

   - Silence the noise so you can hear what your spirit's been trying to tell you.

2. Build a sacred space for thinking.

   - Journal. Meditate. Pray.

   - Give your mind room to breathe and reflect without outside influence.

3. Ask deeper questions.

   - Why do I do this?

- Does this reflect who I really am?

- If nobody could see it, would I still do it?

4. Choose truth-tellers over trendsetters.

   - Surround yourself with people who challenge you to grow, not people who cheer you on toward destruction.

5. Protect your individuality like it's sacred—because it is.

   - Nobody else has your story, your scars, your insight.

   - Don't trade that in for approval you'll regret chasing.

Self-Reflection is a Superpower

There's a reason why most people avoid silence:

Because silence reveals the truth.

And once you hear it... you must choose. You either keep living a lie for the sake of fitting in or you step into your truth and let God show you who you really are. The real you might not be the most popular, but the real you will have peace—and that's something no amount of clout can buy.

Reflection Questions:

1. Where in your life are you being influenced more than you're thinking for yourself?

2. What's one area where you've compromised your values to be accepted?

3. Who in your life truly inspires you to grow—and who only pushes you to go along?

Final Word from Your AUNTIE:

Listen to me, Baby...

You were not created to follow every trend, every voice, every crowd. You were created to think, to lead, to move with intention. Don't let this world convince you that losing your identity is the price you have to pay for luv, friendship, or validation.

The right people will respect your truth.

The wrong ones will reject it.

And either way—you win, because you stayed true to you.

Break the influence.

Reclaim your mind.

And step into the person God already knows you are.

With unshakable Luv,

– AUNTIE Ree

CHAPTER 8:

A.U.N.T.I.E.÷ – Your New Identity Starts Now

"You didn't come this far to play small. You came to shift the atmosphere."

Let's make one thing clear:

This isn't just a book. This is a blueprint.

This isn't about inspiration that fades in a week—it's about transformation that sticks.

Because now that you've made it to the end, I need you to understand something:

You're not the same person who started this journey.

You've dug up old pain.

You've uncovered truth you didn't want to face.

You've stared shame in the eye and started to remember who you really are.

And now?

It's time to live different.

The Full Power of A.U.N.T.I.E.™

This isn't just a cute acronym.

It's the framework that carried me from addiction to assignment,

from brokenness to boldness,

from suicidal to saved,

from confused to called.

Here's what walking in the A.U.N.T.I.E.™ way really looks like:

- Acknowledge Your Feelings – Because numbing pain doesn't erase it. Facing it does.

- Uncover Your Truth – Because lies feel safe, but only truth can set you free.

- Nurture Your Spirit – Because you're not just a body. You're a soul with divine purpose.

- Trust the Process – Because healing isn't linear, but it is worth it.

- Inspire – Because your story has the power to save lives.

- Empower – Because you were born to walk in your authority, not your anxiety.

Every one of these steps is a mirror, a map, a movement and now they belong to you.

This Is Your Permission Slip

Baby, let me say it out loud:

You have permission to grow.

To speak.

To start over.

To heal.

To walk away from toxic people—even if they're family.

To set boundaries.

To rewrite your story.

To step into purpose unapologetically.

To evolve in public—even when they whisper.

To become something greater than what the world expected from you.

This is your permission slip.

Signed by pain.

Stamped by survival.

Sealed by God.

Your Story Isn't Over—It's Just Getting Started

Maybe you've spent years being told who you are...

Too much.

Too quiet.

Too emotional.

Too "churchy."

Too broken.

Too far gone.

But baby, when God rewrites your story, He don't use a pencil. He uses permanent ink.

That means your identity is no longer based on your trauma, your failures, your sexuality, your family, or your past. Your identity is found in the divine design of who God created you to be—before the trauma, before the mistakes, before the world tried to name you.

You are not what happened to you.

You are what you choose to do with it.

The World Needs You Awake and Walking in Purpose

I need you to hear me with your whole spirit:

There are people waiting on the healed version of you.

They're waiting on the bold you.

The you that doesn't flinch when you speak your truth.

The you that doesn't beg to be seen anymore.

The you that walks into every room like you belong there—because you do.

This is the generation that will break generational curses.

This is the generation that will normalize therapy, accountability, prayer, and purpose.

This is the generation that will put respect on healing, not just hustle.

This is the generation that will build legacies out of broken pieces—and show others how to do the same.

You are part of that shift.

Reflection Questions:

1. What chapter or part of your life are you ready to rewrite from a place of healing, not pain?

2. What does it mean for you to walk in the A.U.N.T.I.E.™ way from here on out?

3. Who can you reach back and uplift now that you're learning how to rise?

Final Word from Your AUNTIE:

Baby, I want you to remember something until your last breath. You were never too broken to be used. You were being built. God saw everything—the abuse, the drugs, the shame, the silence, the failed relationships, the thoughts you never told anybody about—and He still called you chosen.

I'm 56, walking in peace and purpose, but I had to go through a whole lot of hell to get here and if all that pain was just so I could reach back and help you avoid yours. It was worth it.

So, walk boldly, speak freely. heal loudly, luv deeply and never again forget the power that's already inside of you. You are not your pain—you are the purpose God preserved through the pain.

Go change the world, Baby. I'll be cheering for you every step of the way.

With everlasting Luv,

– AUNTIE Ree

ACKNOWLEDGMENTS

Shawn Dunham — My Husband, My first best Friend and My Partner for Life! Thank you for loving me unconditionally, yesterday, today and forever more.

To My daughter, Amber Sheree Randolph — My One Luv, your strength and sacrifice inspire me daily. What's understood doesn't have to be explained, but I will say it anyway! You are My #1 Cheerleader and Supporter, Best Friend, Good Good Gurlfriend and our bond is Unbreakable. Thank you for making me a grandmother to the most amazing little human I know.

To my grandson — DaQuan, My "Why" you gave me the courage to rise, speak, and heal out loud. Your life is a living reminder that legacy starts with luv. I will always be your ReeRee and Honey. Luv ya to da moon, stars and beyond.

To my **mother** — There would be no me without you. Thank you for being the best Mother you knew to be with what was given to you. Your Firstborn Daughter with luv always.

To my **small circle of family that became friends and friends who became family** — you know who you are. Thank you for loving me through every chapter. Your encouragement, support, and prayers helped carry me here.

To the little girl I used to be — I see you now. I believe in you. I'm proud of the woman you've become.

And above all, to **God** — Thank you for speaking louder than the voices in my head. Your luv delivered me. Your truth sustained me. Your presence never left me.

CONTACT PAGE

Connect with Sherie (Auntie Ree)

Thank you for taking this journey with me. I'd love to stay connected and support you beyond these pages.

✉@ **Email:** reeteamluv@yahoo.com

🌐 **Website:** www.coachwithauntieree.com

✏ **Speaking Requests:** www.coachwithauntieree.com

🎙 **Podcast:** *Spill and Heal with Auntie Ree*

www.youtube.com/@iamauntieree

📱 **Follow Me:**

IG: @iamauntieree | TikTok @iamauntieree | Facebook: Ree Randolph Dunham | Linkedin: Sherie Randolph-Dunham

Whether you're seeking healing, looking to book me for your next event, or just want to say "Hey Auntie!" — I'd love to hear from you.

Made in the USA
Columbia, SC
06 June 2025